The role of the learning disability worker

Lesley Barcham and Jackie Pountney

Supporting the level 2 and 3 Diplomas in
Health and Social Care (learning disability pathway)
and the Common Induction Standards

Acknowledgements

Photographs from www.careimages.com. Our thanks to Lottie, Choices Housing and Autism Plus for their help.

First published in 2011 jointly by Learning Matters Ltd and the British Institute of Learning Disabilities

All rights reserved. No part of this publication may be reproduced, stored in a retrieval system, or transmitted in any form or by any means, electronic, mechanical, photocopying, recording, or otherwise, without prior permission in writing from Learning Matters.

© 2011 BILD

British Library Cataloguing in Publication Data
A CIP record for this book is available from the British Library

ISBN: 978 0 85725 637 9
This book is also available in the following ebook formats:
Adobe ebook ISBN: 978 0 85725 639 3
EPUB ebook ISBN: 978 0 85725 638 6
Kindle ISBN: 978 0 85725 640 9

The rights of Lesley Barcham and Jackie Pountney to be identified as the authors of this Work have been asserted by them in accordance with the Copyright, Designs and Patents Act 1988.

Cover design by Pentacor
Text design by Pentacor
Project Management by Deer Park Productions
Typeset by Pantek Arts Ltd, Maidstone
Printed and bound in Great Britain by Ashford Colour Press Ltd, Gosport, Hants

Learning Matters Ltd
20 Cathedral Yard
Exeter
EX1 1HB
Tel: 01392 215560
E-mail: info@learningmatters.co.uk
www.learningmatters.co.uk

BILD
Campion House
Green Street
Kidderminster
Worcestershire
DY10 1JL
Tel: 01562 723010
E-mail: enquiries@bild.org.uk
www.bild.org.uk

The role of the learning disability worker

GW 6082102 7

Series Editor: Lesley Barcham

Mandatory Unit and Common Induction Standards titles

Communicating effectively with people with a learning disability
ISBN 978 0 85725 510 5

Personal development for learning disability workers ISBN 978 0 85725 609 6

Equality and inclusion for learning disability workers ISBN 978 0 85725 514 3

Duty of care for learning disability workers ISBN 978 0 85725 613 3

Principles of safeguarding and protection for learning disability workers
ISBN 978 0 85725 506 8

Person centred approaches when supporting people with a learning disability
ISBN 978 0 85725 625 6

The role of the learning disability worker ISBN 978 0 85725 637 9

Contents

This book covers:

- Common Induction Standards – Standard 1 – Role of the health and social care worker (excluding Learning Outcome 4, which is covered in the book *Handling information for learning disability workers* in this series)

- Level 2 and Level 3 diploma unit HSC 025 – The role of the health and social care worker

---

Llyfrgelloedd Mon, Conwy & Gwynedd Libraries	
GW 6082102 7	
ASKEWS & HOLT	
	£12.99
KW	

About the authors and the people who contributed to this book

Julie Smith and Getta Life

Julie Smith is one of two directors who set up, and now manage, Getta Life. Julie has worked with people with learning difficulties for many years in various settings, and is passionate about people being valued and supported in a 'person centred way'. Getta Life is a small organisation supporting people with more complex needs to live in their own homes and to live the life they choose. It works through person centred approaches, providing small individualised teams who build relationships with individuals and get to know each other well.

Tina and James Cooper

James lives in his own bungalow in the West Midlands and leads a full life in the community and with his family. He receives 24 hour support from a day service, a local care provider and his family. James loves swimming, music, going out to eat, watching football and motor racing. James' mother Tina was his main carer when he lived at home, until three years ago. Tina and the rest of the family supported James to get his own home and arrange his support using a personal budget. Tina has supported other people with learning disabilities and their family carers to get a good life through self directed support. Tina is a director of Time4People, an organisation that provides information, training and consultancy on all aspects of personalisation. For more information go to www.time4people.org.uk

Lesley Barcham

Lesley's career has been about learning. She trained as a teacher of deaf children in the 1970s and started out as a hearing therapist and then teacher of secondary aged deaf children. She has also worked in residential child care, as a teacher of children and adults with a learning disability in a further education college. Lesley gained a PhD from the Open University in the 1990s for her research into the development of education for disabled children in Southern Africa. Lesley has worked for BILD for 14 years on a variety of learning materials and programmes. From 2009 – 2011 she was seconded part time to the Valuing People Team as workforce adviser.

Jackie Pountney

Jackie has worked at BILD since 2004, where she supports organisations to offer learning disability qualifications to their staff. Before this she worked with people with learning disabilities, first with Birmingham social services department, and later in a further education college. She has co-authored *Not behind the bikeshed,* a resource pack for teaching health and personal education to people with learning disabilities, and was the author of the BILD publications, *Your role as a learning disability worker* and *Protecting people who have a learning disability from abuse.*

Introduction

Who is this book for?

The Role of the Learning Disability Worker is for you if you:

- have a new job working with people with learning disabilities with a support provider or as a personal assistant;
- are a more experienced worker who is studying for a qualification for your own professional development or are seeking more information to improve your practice;
- are a volunteer supporting people with a learning disability;
- are a manager in a service supporting people with a learning disability and you have training or supervisory responsibility for the induction of new workers and the continuous professional development of more experienced staff;
- if you are a direct payment or personal budget user and are planning the induction or training for your personal assistant.

Links to qualifications and the Common Induction Standards

This book gives you all the information you need to complete both one of the Common Induction Standards and the unit on the role of the learning disability worker from the level 2 and level 3 diplomas in health and social care. You may use the learning from this unit in a number of ways:

- to help you complete the Common Induction Standards;
- to work towards a full qualification e.g. the level 2 or level 3 diploma in health and social care;
- as learning for the unit on the role of the learning disability worker for your professional development.

This unit is one of the mandatory units that everyone doing the full level 2 and level 3 diploma must study. Although anyone studying for the qualifications will find the book useful, it is particularly helpful for people who support a person with a learning disability. The messages and stories used in this book are from people with a learning disability, family carers and people working with them.

Links to assessment

If you are studying for this unit and want to gain accreditation towards a qualification, first of all you will need to make sure that you are registered with an awarding organisation who offers the qualification. Then you will need to provide a portfolio of evidence for assessment. The person responsible for training within your organisation will advise you about registering with an awarding organisation and give you information about the type of evidence you will need to provide for assessment. You can also get additional information from BILD. For more information about qualifications and assessment, please go to the BILD website: www.bild.org.uk/qualifications

How this book is organised

Generally each chapter covers one learning outcome from the qualification unit, and one of the Common Induction Standards. The learning outcomes covered are clearly highlighted at the beginning of each chapter. Each chapter starts with a story from a person with a learning disability or family carer or worker. This introduces the topic and is intended to help you think about the topic from their point of view. Each chapter contains:

Thinking points – to help you reflect on your practice;

Stories – examples of good support from people with learning disabilities and family carers;

Activities – for you to use to help you to think about your work with people with learning disabilities;

Key points – a summary of the main messages in that chapter;

References and where to go for more information – useful references to help further study.

At the end of the book there is:

A glossary – explaining specialist language in plain English;

An index – to help you look up a particular topic easily.

Study skills

Studying for a qualification can be very rewarding. However, it can be daunting if you have not studied for a long time, or are wondering how to fit your studies into an already busy life. The BILD website contains lots of advice to help you to study successfully, including information about effective reading, taking notes, organising your time, using the internet for research. For further information, go to www.bild.org.uk/qualifications

Chapter 1

Understanding working relationships when supporting people with a learning disability

James has lots of different people supporting him, in his home, out in the community, at the day service and people who support him with his various health needs. Also his family are an important part of his life. For James to stay safe and healthy it is important that we all work together and share information. Because James has a number of health needs it is really important that people follow his support plan and let other workers know if things are OK or if there is a problem. Support workers in one setting need to know about the other people who support James and how to communicate with them. Good workers respect the experience of his family – they listen to us and pass important information on to us.

Tina Cooper – mother of James

Introduction

At the heart of your work with people with a learning disability is developing and maintaining relationships. As well as providing good support for the person with a learning disability that you are employed to work with, you will probably also be working with a number of other people. The other people you may have a working relationship with include family members and friends of the person you support, your work colleagues, your supervisor or manager and other people from your organisation, as well as workers from other organisations.

It is therefore important to understand the working relationships you will be involved in as part of your role as a learning disability worker. This chapter will help you to think about the different types of working relationships, your responsibilities to the people you work with and in particular your main responsibilities to the individual or individuals you support.

Learning outcomes

This chapter will help you to:

- understand your main responsibilities to an individual you support;
- explain how your relationship with an individual you support is different from other working and personal relationships;
- describe the different working relationships in health and social care.

This chapter covers:

- Common Induction Standards – Standard 1 – Role of the health and social care worker: Learning Outcome 1
- Level 2 HSC 025 – The role of the health and social care worker: Learning Outcome 1

Your responsibilities to an individual you support

At the heart of your work with people with a learning disability is developing and maintaining relationships.

When you start to work with a person with a learning disability it can feel quite overwhelming trying to get to grips with what exactly your responsibilities are. You don't want to do anything wrong or forget something. It is important therefore to have a clear understanding of your responsibilities to the people you support.

Activity

Over the next two or three days, as you carry out your job supporting a person with a learning disability, think about what your main responsibilities are to that person. Write a list of all the responsibilities to them that you think you have. Discuss your list with your line manager at your next supervision.

Even if you are an experienced worker and you have worked for the same organisation, in the same setting, with the same people for some time, your job has probably changed over the years. Your responsibilities might have changed because:

- the needs of the person you support have changed;
- the way the service is delivered has changed;
- the policies and procedures have changed;
- you have developed in your role, undertaken training and taken on new responsibilities.

You can find out about your responsibilities to the people you support in a number of different places.

Your responsibilities to the people with learning disabilities that you support, their family members, your colleagues and workers from partner organisations are set out in several places including:

Your job description and contract of employment – these should clearly set out the main reason for your role, your main responsibilities, where you will be working, who you will be supervised by and the people you will be working with as well as any other duties you may be asked to carry out.

The aims and objectives of the organisation you work for – these guide you in relation to the values of the organisation, and they will influence how all the staff are expected to conduct themselves. See Chapter 2 for more information on this topic.

The person's support plan or care plan – most people with a learning disability have a support plan or care plan that gives information about how they want to be supported. Many support plans are quite detailed, for example giving information about communication, personal care needs, healthcare tasks or the person's daily routines. You have a responsibility to read and implement the parts of the support plan that relate to your role.

The policies and procedures of your organisation or the agreed ways of working with your employer – these give information about how you should behave and work in particular situations, for example in relation to confidentiality, safeguarding and protection issues, health and safety and lots of other areas. There is more information on this in Chapter 2. The policies and procedures give details about what your responsibilities are in particular situations.

The national laws and policies – many of the responsibilities of learning disability workers are directly related to national laws and policies. For example, the Health and Safety at Work Act informs your employer's health and safety policy, and the Human Rights Act and the Equality Act inform the equalities policy. By following the policies and procedures of your organisation you will be keeping within the law as the policies and procedures should be taken from national laws and should be regularly updated to reflect any legal changes.

The Code of Practice for Social Care Workers – as well as having responsibilities towards the people you support and the organisation that employs you, you also have wider responsibilities as one of over a million social care workers in the UK. The social care councils for each of the four countries of the UK were set up by the government in 2001 to register and regulate all social care workers. The General Social Care Council, the Care Council for Wales, the Northern Ireland Social Care Council and the Scottish Social Services Council all published *Codes of Practice for Social Care Workers* in 2002.

You should always work to the standards set out in the Code of Practice. This sets out standards relating to professional conduct and practice that are required of social care workers. You will find that many of these standards are similar to those from your own organisation, but the difference is that these are set at a national level and have been devised to ensure people who are supported, their families, carers and other members of the public know the standards of conduct they should expect from social care workers.

In particular, in relation to your responsibilities as a learning disability worker, the Code says '... workers must strive to establish and maintain the trust and confidence of service users and carers. This includes:

- being honest and trustworthy;
- communicating in an appropriate, open, accurate and straightforward way;
- respecting confidential information ...;
- being reliable and dependable;
- honouring work commitments ... and when it is not possible to do so, explaining why to service users and carers;
- declaring issues that might create a conflict of interest ...;
- adhering to policies and procedures about accepting gifts and money ...'

The Code of Practice also says that 'you must not:

- exploit service users, carers and colleagues;
- form inappropriate personal relationships with service users.'

For more information about the Code of Practice see the references section at the end of this chapter.

Activity

Read your job description and contract of employment carefully. Note down all the responsibilities you have in your job, and also who you are accountable to. If you don't have a job description or a contract of employment then talk to your line manager immediately about this.

Next, share your list with your line manager or employer. Check that all your responsibilities are covered in the list. If your job description is out of date or if you are unsure about anything make sure that you talk about this too.

How is your relationship with an individual you support different from other working and personal relationships?

Every one of our relationships is different, but it can be helpful to think about some of the different types of relationships you have in your life before you consider your relationship with the people you support. Here are some of the main types of relationships you are likely to have in your life:

Your close and intimate relationships – this group might include your partner, close family and your best friends. With this group of people you can be yourself and you feel accepted for who you are. You can share your hopes, fears and dreams with them. With these people you have a strong mutual commitment to supporting each other through good and bad times.

Your friends – this group could include people you have known for many years or those you have got to know more recently. Your relationship with your friends is usually based on a shared common interest and because you enjoy each other's company. With your friends you may share a particular interest, say for a football team, a hobby or a political or religious affiliation. Your relationship with your friends is usually mutually supportive, but you may not share all the details of your personal life with all of your friends.

Your acquaintances – these are people you may see regularly or infrequently who you may pass the time of day with, but who mostly don't know you very well. Many of us have acquaintances that we meet in the local shop, when we are out walking the dog or who provide us with occasional services, such as a hairdresser. Increasingly people also have virtual friends and acquaintances who are people they know only through online communities or social networks. Again these are voluntary relationships.

Your work relationships – this group includes the people you support and their family carers, and colleagues who work for the same employer as you. It might include people from other organisations who are also involved in the life of a person you support, for example a district nurse or job coach. In these relationships you are bound by a contract of employment and a professional Code of Practice. These are relationships that you enter into as part of your paid work. You are paid to develop a good working relationship with people and although often these are strong reciprocal relationships, occasionally you will need to develop a relationship with a person you find harder to get on with.

> *Think about the range of different relationships you have in your life. You might want to think about them using the four groups outlined above. Think about the key people in each group.*

In some ways your relationship with the person you support will be similar to other relationships in your life – you probably get on with some people very well; you may find others harder to like. The people you support may get on well with some support workers and not very well with others. However, in other ways your relationship with the person you support is very different.

Many people with learning disabilities spend a substantial amount of time with people who are paid to be with them and they may share a lot of personal information with those people. One result of this is that many individuals with learning disabilities regard the people who support them as their friends. While this may be flattering for you as a support worker, and may help you both to have a good relationship, you should remember that you also have a professional relationship with the people you support.

Having a professional relationship with a person with learning disabilities and their family carers means:

- respecting and valuing them at all times;
- listening to people and trying to understand their perspective;
- working in a inclusive way that celebrates diversity and every person's contribution;
- recognising and upholding the rights of every person with learning disabilities;
- promoting the person's independence and not doing everything for them or taking over all responsibilities;
- recognising people's right to control their own lives, so long as it does not affect the freedom of others;
- remembering you have a duty of care towards the people you support;
- being reliable and dependable;
- not developing inappropriate relationships with the people you support.

At the heart of your work with people with a learning disability is developing and maintaining relationships.

As you can see from the information from Tina and James Cooper at the beginning of this chapter, good communication is essential in building good working relationships. It's important that you develop a good relationship with the person you support as this relationship is crucial to providing the support you are employed to provide. Good communication is a key element of developing a good working relationship between you and the person you support. In the book, *Communicating Effectively with People with a Learning Disability* in this series, you can find out more about how you can build good relationships on the foundation of good communication.

Your relationship with the person you support is different from other relationships because you:

- are employed to provide support and your contract of employment sets out in detail the nature of that support;

- have a duty of care;

- are bound by the professional *Code of Practice for Social Care Workers*;

- will move in and out of the person's life.

Although as members of society we all have a general 'duty of care' to others, you have additional responsibilities in relation to 'duty of care' as a support worker. You can find out more about duty of care in the book *Duty of Care for Learning Disability Workers* in this series.

What are the different working relationships in health and social care?

Activity

For the next three days when you are supporting a person with a learning disability make a list of all of the people you have a working relationship with. Then put the people under one of the following four headings:

- *People I support.*
- *Family carers and friends of the people I support.*
- *Colleagues from the organisation I work for.*
- *Workers from other organisations.*

Review your list with a colleague. Have you missed anyone out? Talk about any differences you see in the relationships you have with the people in the four groups.

Many people with a learning disability have relationships with paid workers from a number of different organisations. These might include people who support them in their home, those who support them in daytime activities or in their work, as well as professionals who help in particular areas of their life, for example with healthcare support such as their GP, an epilepsy consultant and nurse, their job coach, etc.

Look at the diagram below that shows the network of relationships that Lottie has with a number of different people. These include people from the four groups above. You can read more about good communication with work colleagues in the book *Communicating Effectively with People with a Learning Disability* in this series. It is likely that the people you support will have a similar network of relationships. However, their network may be quite different from your own, with more people in a relationship with them in a working capacity and a smaller number of close friends and acquaintances.

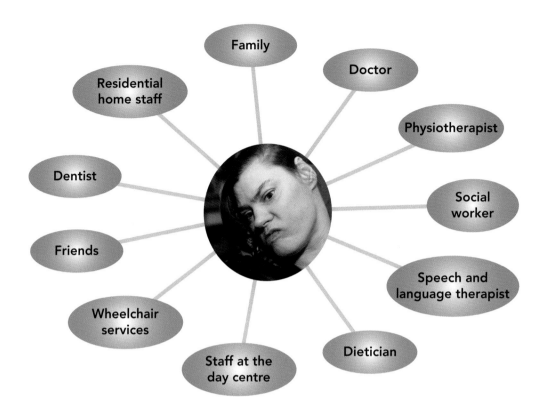

Example of people working with Lottie.

Some of the different relationships you might experience in your work supporting people with a learning disability	Your responsibilities in this relationship could include:
Family members and friends of the person	• treating people with dignity and respect • listening carefully to their views and contributions • communicating effectively with them • ensuring consistent support
Colleagues who do the same or very similar work to you	• communicating effectively with them about the support you are providing • working cooperatively with them to provide good support

Your supervisor or line manager	<ul><li>reporting to them any problems or difficulties you are having</li><li>clarifying your responsibilities</li><li>preparing for and attending your supervisions and appraisals</li><li>asking for information about policies or procedures</li></ul>
The key worker of a person you support	<ul><li>seeking information about an aspect of the person's support</li><li>reporting to them about the person's support</li></ul>
The person's advocate	<ul><li>supporting the advocacy relationship</li><li>supporting the person's rights and choices</li><li>communicating effectively</li></ul>
Workers from other parts of your organisation	<ul><li>providing or receiving information on a particular issue, e.g. in relation to your contract of employment, risk management, specialist areas such as communication</li><li>working in partnership with them on a project or a person's support</li></ul>
Workers from other organisations supporting the person	<ul><li>exchanging information about the person's support</li><li>seeking advice and information</li><li>arranging meetings or appointments</li><li>working in partnership on a project or in relation to a person's support</li></ul>
Other people in mainstream organisations, e.g. leisure centre, town hall	<ul><li>finding out or providing information on behalf of the person you support</li><li>supporting the person while they are using their service</li><li>promoting inclusive practice and the rights of the person you support when necessary</li></ul>

In all your relationships with others when you are supporting a person with a learning disability you need to keep in mind the standards of conduct set out in the *Code of Practice for Social Care Workers*. The Code of Practice says the following about your different working relationships with family members and other workers:

You must not:

- abuse, neglect or harm service users, carers or colleagues;
- discriminate unlawfully or unjustifiably against service users, carers and colleagues;
- condone any unlawful or unjustifiable discrimination by service users, carers or colleagues.

You must:

- work openly and cooperatively with colleagues and treat them with respect;
- recognise and respect the roles and expertise of workers from other agencies and work in partnership with them.

Key points from this chapter

- You can find information about your responsibilities towards the people you support in the *Code of Practice for Social Care Workers*, in your job description and in the policies and procedures of your organisation.

- Working relationships are different from the other relationships in your life because you are paid to develop and maintain the relationship and you are bound by the policies and procedures of your organisation and a professional code of practice.

- As a learning disability worker you will be involved in a number of different working relationships including those with family members, advocates and colleagues from your own and other organisations.

- In your working relationship you must work openly and cooperatively with colleagues and treat them with respect. You must recognise and respect the roles and expertise of workers from other agencies.

References and where to go for more information

References

Barksby, J and Harper, L (2011) *Duty of Care for Learning Disability Workers.* Exeter: Learning Matters and BILD

GSCC (2001) *Code of Practice for Social Care Workers,* downloadable from www.gscc.org.uk

SCIE (2010) *Forming and Maintaining Relationships with Service Users, Professionals and Others,* free e-learning course downloadable from www.scie.org.uk

SENSE (2009) *Personal and Professional Relationships,* autumn/winter 2009, downloadable from www.sense.org.uk

Thurman, S (2011) *Communicating Effectively for Learning Disability Workers.* Exeter: Learning Matters and BILD

Websites

PANET Personal Assistant Network www.panet.org.uk

Skills for Care www.skillsforcare.org.uk

The Social Care Councils (responsible for the regulation and registration of Social Workers and other Social Care Workers) are:

General Social Care Council (England) www.gscc.org.uk

Care Council for Wales www.ccwales.org.uk

Northern Ireland Social Care Council www.niscc.info

Scottish Social Services Council www.sssc.uk.com

Chapter 2

Working in ways that are agreed with your employer

I was put in a difficult situation really, and at first I didn't know what to do. We were short staffed and the new senior support worker was very busy. She asked me to do the medication with Emma and Jeannie as she was about to take Faye to the day centre. I knew lots about the medication and had watched others sort out the pills, but it was only the seniors who could do the medication. I really wanted to be helpful, but I couldn't do something that might harm Emma or Jeannie. So I told the senior worker I couldn't as it wasn't part of my job role and I hadn't been trained to do it. But I could take Faye to the day centre as I had been on the bus with her before.

Annie, a support worker

Introduction

In this chapter we explore the other important factors that you need to consider when trying to understand your role as a learning disability worker. These include knowing how your day-to-day work for an organisation fits into its wider aims and objectives, and knowing about and following the policies and procedures. This chapter also looks at why it is necessary for learning disability workers to understand and keep within their job role.

Learning outcomes

This chapter will help you to:

- understand the aims, objectives and values of the organisation you work for;
- know why it is important to adhere to the agreed scope of the job role;

- explain why it is important to work in ways agreed with your employer;
- access and implement the policies and procedures or agreed ways of working.

This chapter covers:

- Common Induction Standards – Standard 1 – Role of the health and social care worker: Learning Outcome 2
- Level 2 HSC 025 – The role of the health and social care worker: Learning Outcome 2

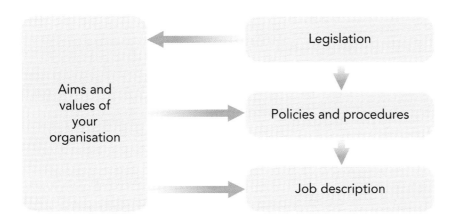

Understanding the factors that influence your job role.

The aims and values of your organisation

As well as understanding your role and responsibilities it's important to look at the aims and values of your organisation. When you understand what these mean it can be easier to see how your day-to-day contribution helps your organisation work towards its goals.

Every organisation has a set of aims and values. You should have been given information about them at your interview and talked about them during your induction. Have you really thought about what they mean, and how they help you do your job?

An aim is a general statement of what an organisation hopes to achieve in its work with people with learning disabilities. Some organisations put their aims into a mission statement or a vision so find out if your organisation uses these terms. Values are statements about what an organisation considers to be important in its work with people with learning disabilities. They are the expression of the principles on which the organisation was founded and underpin the way that it operates. Values inform the aims of an organisation.

Here are some statements about the aims of some organisations that support people with a learning disability, taken from their websites (some have been slightly adapted). You can easily find out information about different organisations by looking on their website or in their annual review.

These are some of the aims of different organisations:

- To support people who have a learning disability to live as independently as possible.
- We believe in high quality, good value support wherever we provide it. Rights, independence, choice and inclusion are central to all we do.
- To value and support people with a learning disability and their families.
- To provide support in the way people want it when they want it.
- To put an individual's own strengths and abilities at the centre of their support.

These are some statements about the values of different organisations:

- All people are individuals and everyone's unique qualities, abilities and experience are valuable assets.
- People are resourceful and have the potential for developmental growth.
- People have the right to take risks and to receive support to safely exercise this choice.
- All people are of equal value.
- Being person centred.
- We make things possible by working together, understanding, determination, building a sustainable business.
- We aim to be respectful, supportive, inclusive and responsive.
- To support our mission we will be empowering, respectful, imaginative and professional.

- Empowering, including and respecting people.
- Everyone has the potential to develop knowledge and learn new skills.
- Everyone should be allowed equal access to education, training, employment and access to the facilities in the community.
- To support people with learning difficulties to reach their full potential and fully participate in the life of the community.

Thinking point

What similarities can you see between the aims and values above? Are there many differences?

You can see from these examples that there are quite a few similarities in the values of different organisations. You will also see that the aims are fairly broad. Although they do not tell us very much about the day-to-day activities of the organisation, they do give some clues about what kind of values would be expected to underpin the daily work of their staff.

MacIntyre is a provider of services for people with a learning disability. In a recent book *Great Interactions* (2011), describing a project to improve the communication and interactions between the staff and the people they support, Bill Mumford, their managing director, says of the values of the organisation that 'people don't experience our values, they experience our behaviours'. Our values and attitudes need to influence our behaviour. At MacIntyre the project was an important way for all the workers to reflect on how the customers of their services, the people they support, were experiencing the values of the organisation.

Activity

Find and read a copy of the aims and values of your organisation. List three ways in which you can promote its aims and values through your day-to-day work. Does your behaviour at work reflect the values of the organisation? When you have completed this activity discuss it with your line manager or supervisor.

If you are working as a personal assistant employed by one person you are unlikely to have information on the aims and objectives of an organisation, but what you might well have, if the person wants to share them with you, is a copy of all or part of their person centred plan as well as their support plan. These should direct you with your values and give important information about the person's aims in life. Your work is to support them in achieving their aims.

Find out about the aims and values of your organisation.

Thinking point

If you support an individual within their own family think about how you could promote the values that are important to that person and their family carers in the way you work.

Why is it important to keep to the agreed scope of the job role?

In the story at the beginning of the chapter you can see how Annie responded when she was asked to do something that wasn't in her job role and that she wasn't trained to do. In Chapter 1 you looked at your job description and your main responsibilities to the people you support and the other people you work with in your job. Your job description provides the information you need about the scope of your job role. When you start work supporting people with a learning disability your employer will arrange an induction programme for you. This will usually involve some on the job training as well as some more formal training. At the beginning you may not be able to do all of the tasks set out in your job description, but your training will help you to build up the skills and knowledge you will require. In your supervision sessions with your line manager you will need to agree a personal development plan for you to learn all aspects of your job.

Whether you are a new or experienced worker it is important to keep to the agreed scope of your job role as set out in your job description for a number of reasons:

- The people you support and their families need the confidence of knowing that either their personal assistant or the organisation providing the support is able to meet their needs as set out in their support plan.

- Your employer has written the job descriptions for you and your colleagues to ensure that all the tasks needed to provide good support are covered. If you are not carrying out all of the tasks in your job description then it is possible that part of the support for the people you work with could be missed.

- It sets out the limit of your responsibility and it helps you and others recognise the tasks you are and are not allowed to do. This protects the people you support from possible harm as well as protecting you and your organisation.

- It decreases the risk of harm to you and all the people you work with, as undertaking a task that is not in your job description and that you have not been trained to do could lead to greater risks for all involved.

- Understanding the scope of your role and regularly reviewing your job description with your line manager will help you to identify any training needs you may have.

- In most organisations workers have a regular appraisal of their work. Most organisations evaluate their workers' performance against their job description so it is important to make sure your job description is up to date and reflects all of the tasks that you do.

- When working in partnership with others, if you and the colleagues involved share the scope of your job roles this will give you clarity about each other's main responsibilities. This will help you to identify if any important tasks are not being covered by anyone in the team.

Why is it important to work in ways agreed with your employer?

If you work for an organisation that provides care and support for people you will find your employer's agreed ways of working in the organisation's policies and procedures. These policies and procedures describe the right way to carry out particular tasks. Policies set out an organisation's position on a particular issue and offer guidance on what to do. Policies explain how the organisation will respond to national legislation to ensure that both the organisation and its staff work within the law. Procedures give practical guidance on how a policy should be implemented and explain in more detail what workers should do in response to a specific situation.

So, for example, your organisation should have a policy on confidentiality. This will explain the reasons for confidentiality, the laws on data protection that directly influence what should and should not be done, and the organisation's commitment to maintaining confidential information. The procedures will show you and other workers how you should deliver the policy in your daily work. For example, the procedures will tell you:

- what information you can give to others;
- how you must store records and files;
- what to do in case of a breach of confidentiality;
- where to get additional information if you are unsure what to do.

Policies and procedures can usually be found in the staff handbook or on the organisation's intranet, and copies of policies and procedures can then be downloaded from there. Every member of staff should have a copy, or should know where a copy is kept. In many organisations workers need to sign a form to say that they have received a copy of the handbook, have read it and confirm that they will follow it.

Supervisors and managers need to be sure that every member of staff is aware of all the policies and procedures relating to their work. As a new member of staff it is your job to find out about policies and procedures and to check with your manager if there is anything you don't fully understand. As an experienced member of staff you need to keep up to date with any changes to the policies and procedures.

As a new member of staff it is your job to find out about policies and procedures.

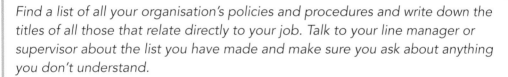

Activity

Find a list of all your organisation's policies and procedures and write down the titles of all those that relate directly to your job. Talk to your line manager or supervisor about the list you have made and make sure you ask about anything you don't understand.

If you are employed by a person who has a direct payment or personal budget and uses their money to employ their own personal assistants then you may not have all of the policies and procedures that a care provider might have. Instead your employer may have set out in your contract of employment, or in your job description or in their support plan, the ways they want you to work. As a personal assistant, if you need to find out exactly what you should do in a particular situation you will need to:

- check in your job description and contract of employment;

- discuss with your employer the ways they want you to work;

- make a record of your discussion so that you can refer to it at a later date.

Remember as a personal assistant you must always work within the law and also the standards set out in the *Code of Practice for Social Care Workers.*

Activity

If you are a personal assistant directly employed by the person with a learning disability or their family, talk to them about the details of how they want you to work. It might be helpful to focus on issues that affect your daily work – for example, the agreed ways of working relating to managing the person's money, managing risk or ways of managing challenging behaviour. How do you find this out? What do you do if you are unsure about what you should do?

Accessing and implementing policies and procedures or agreed ways of working

When you work supporting people with a learning disability every day is different so you can't always predict when you might need to refer to one of the policies or procedures or the agreed ways of working. It is important therefore to know:

- about all the policies and procedures that relate to your work;
- where to go to find the policies and procedures when you need them;
- who to go to if you have any questions or concerns.

In many organisations each member of staff is given their own copy of the policies and procedures and you may be required to sign to say you have read and understood them and that you will follow them. Is this your experience?

Activity

Imagine that over the next week you experience one or all of the following five situations:

1. *You are offered an expensive gift by a family carer with whom you have been working recently.*
2. *You and the person you support are involved in a minor accident while driving to visit their friend.*
3. *The person you support tells you that a valuable watch that their grandfather had given them has gone from their room, and they think one of your colleagues might have stolen it.*

4. *The college tutor of the person you support rings you and asks for confidential medical information.*

5. *You are told by the neighbour of a person you support that someone else in their block of flats is getting too friendly with them.*

For each of these situations think about which policy you should be looking through for guidance about what you should do. Discuss your ideas with your manager.

It is not only the employees of an organisation who need to know about the policies and procedures. The people with a learning disability who are supported by the organisation and their family carers also need to know about them and they need to have access to them in a way that is best for them. The people you support might want information about the policies as an Easy Read document or to have an audio file. Family carers also need details about how the organisation will manage certain situations. Part of your role as a learning disability worker is to make sure that people know how certain situations will be managed and that they are provided with the information in a way that is most suitable for them.

Implementing the policies and procedures

It is important for social care workers not only to know about the policies and procedures of the organisation they work for, but also to implement them. Once you have read the policies and procedures or agreed ways of working to help you in a particular situation it is important that you then follow them. It is important to implement the policies and procedures fully because if you don't you may:

- put the person you support at risk of harm;

- put yourself or a colleague at risk of harm;

- be subject to a disciplinary process because your contract of employment says that you must follow them;

- damage the reputation of the organisation you work for, and if the matter is serious it could result in an investigation by the social care inspectors or the police.

Activity

Look at the five examples on page 22 of situations you might experience in your day-to-day work. If these situations happened to you and you failed to implement the policies and procedures as you ought to do what might be the consequences:

- *for the person you support?*
- *for you?*
- *for your organisation?*

Discuss your ideas with your line manager or at your next team meeting.

Key points from this chapter

- For learning disability workers employed by an organisation it is important to know the aims and objectives of the organisation and to reflect on how these directly affect your work.

- You need to keep to the scope of your job role so that you can provide high quality, safe support to the people you work with.

- It is your responsibility to be sure you fully understand all of the policies and procedures, or agreed ways of working, which relate to your job.

- If you are unsure what to do in a particular situation refer to the policies and procedures or agreed ways of working. If you are still unsure, ask your manager for advice and support.

- You must implement the policies and procedures. If you don't you may put the person you support and others at risk, you may be breaking the law and you may damage the reputation of your employer.

References and where to go for more information

References

Crowther, C, Mumford, B and McFadzean, G (2011) *Great Interactions – It ain't what you do it's the way that you do it.* Milton Keynes: MacIntyre, downloadable from www.macintyrecharity.org

Websites

PANET Personal Assistant Network www.panet.org.uk

Skills for Care www.skillsforcare.org.uk

The Social Care Councils (responsible for the regulation and registration of Social Workers and other Social Care Workers) are:

General Social Care Council (England) www.gscc.org.uk

Care Council for Wales www.ccwales.org.uk

Northern Ireland Social Care Council www.niscc.info

Scottish Social Services Council www.sssc.uk.com

Chapter 3

Working in partnership with others

> It is very important to us at Getta Life that all of our staff work in partnership with the family carers of the people we support. Developing and maintaining positive relationships with the people we support, their families and staff from other organisations is a priority. We teach all of our new staff that 'your job is about relationships. We want you to focus on having good relationships with all the people you work with.'
>
> Mostly these relationships go well but sometimes there are misunderstandings and conflicts. In team meetings and supervision we all try to reflect on what has gone well and we celebrate; and then if things don't go so well we reflect on the experience and look for creative solutions with the people involved. We need our staff to be able to put themselves in the other person's shoes and be non critical in their approach.
>
> *Julie Smith – Getta Life*

Introduction

In your work you will probably come into contact with a wide variety of people at different times. Obviously, your main relationship is with the person with a learning disability you support, but you may also work with members of the person's family, their friends, other support workers and professionals, and people in the person's wider circle of contacts from their work or leisure and social activities.

When you begin your new role supporting a person with a learning disability you may find that there are a variety of people who also support the same person, but in different ways. It is important that you understand the roles and responsibilities of all those involved in the person's life and the different relationships that you will need to establish with them. Partnership working will be important in your work.

Learning outcomes

This chapter will help you to:

- understand the importance of working in partnership with carers, families, advocates and others significant to the person;

- recognise why it is important to work in teams and in partnership with others;

- understand how to improve partnership working;

- identify skills and approaches to resolve conflicts;

- know where, how and when to access support and advice about partnership working or resolving conflicts.

This chapter covers:

- Common Induction Standards – Standard 1 – Role of the health and social care worker: Learning Outcome 3

- Level 2 diploma HSC 025 – The role of the health and social care worker: Learning Outcome 3

Understanding the importance of working in partnership with carers, families, advocates and others significant to the person

Partnership working is important in social care work so that people with learning disabilities get good consistent support. If you look again at the message from Tina and James Cooper on page 1 at the beginning of Chapter 1 you can see how important it is for people to work together so that James stays safe and healthy and has a good life.

Family members and close friends of people with learning disabilities are particularly important when we think about partnership working. For example, *Valuing People Now* (2009), the Government's three-year strategy to improve the lives of people with learning disabilities and their families in England, says that:

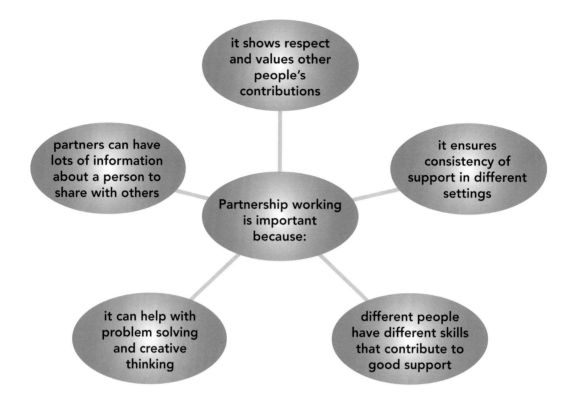

Families are at the heart of Valuing People Now. When we use the term 'family' we are including everyone in the family; including people with learning disabilities. No two families are the same and they come in all shapes and sizes but when we speak to families most of them tell us that three things are very important:

- getting the best life possible for their family member with a learning disability;

- for other people to recognise and value the role of families and to work in partnership with them; and

- for family carers to get the help and support they need to live a good life.

In fact, the right to respect for private and family life is a human right under the Human Rights Act 1998.

The work of Skills for Care on *Carers Matter – Everybody's Business* has also highlighted the vital role that health and social care workers play in ensuring that family carers are treated as equal partners and as experts in the delivery of care.

Common Core Principles for Working with Carers (Skills for Care, 2010) sets out eight principles that social care workers should use to develop their practice.

These are the common core principles for working with family carers:

- Carers are equal partners in care. Recognise that over time, carers become experts with skills that are to be valued and appreciated.
- Make no assumptions regarding a carer's capacity or carers' capacities and willingness to take responsibility for, or to continue to, care.
- Support carers to be physically and mentally as well as possible and prevent ill health.
- Work together to involve all carers in decision making.
- Provide care and support with flexibility and understanding in personalised ways that reflect the circumstances, cultural background and lifestyle of the carer and person cared for.
- Respect and recognise that carers will have their own support needs, rights and aspirations, which may be different from that of the cared for person.
- Identify, support and enable children and young people who are carers to be children and young people as well as carers.
- Recognise the experience of carers as the caring role ends and after it has ended and offer support to carers accordingly.

For more information go to www.skillsforcare.org.uk

In the book *Partnership Working with Family Carers of People with Learning Disabilities and People with Autistic Spectrum Conditions* in this series, Alison Cowen and Jamie Hanson identify four ways in which support workers can work well in partnership with families. They call this the 4Rs. The information below is taken from their book. It highlights the qualities needed to work well in partnership with families.

The 4 Rs

- Respect
- Recognition
- Reassurance
- Rapport

1. Respect

Working with respect and genuine interest with family members is essential. They will have supported and cared for their son or daughter before you entered their life and probably will continue to do so afterwards, when you no longer work with them. Siblings may be the person's lifelong supporter, closest to them in age, even if their involvement is not on a day-to-day basis.

There is an old adage that 'you have to earn respect'. It is reasonable to say that a parent who has supported and cared for their son or daughter with learning disabilities into adulthood has, for a variety of reasons, earned respect.

One way of showing and earning respect can be by listening to their point of view. This creates opportunities for the family members to share their beliefs and values. Many family members may have struggled for many years to have their opinions listened to by professionals and in turn may have felt disrespected.

2. Recognition

Recognition is to acknowledge something. It seems such a simple thing yet holds a great importance for most of us – family members in particular, whose efforts may go unrecognised and where families may support their relative at a hidden cost.

When the person they have supported and cared for over a lifetime moves on, family members' past and present contributions may not be fully recognised by paid staff. This is not only disrespectful but a waste of a huge resource that could be used to provide quality and meaningful support to the individual.

So what is it you are recognising?

Recognise the journey – the family member and the person you support have been on a journey of experience. Some experiences have been positive and some have been negative, but either way a lot of learning has been gained. Recognising this journey not only respects the family member, it also gives access to a lifetime of knowledge that can support you to support the individual.

Recognise the relationship – the relationship between the family member and the individual has existed, in most cases, all of the person's life. Recognising the importance and the longevity of the relationship is vital. Like many family relationships there will be a certain level of interdependence between the parties. Some parts of the relationship you may view as negative while others you may see as positive. Sometimes you will come across situations that happen between a person and a family member that do not seem right and you may want to intervene. Before you do, ask yourself how this would affect their relationship.

3. Reassurance

After a lifetime of caring and supporting their son or daughter, a family member will want to be sure that they are getting what's best for them from paid staff. The reassurance they need will differ between different families' attitudes and lifestyles. But reassurance is about letting people know that you understand their circumstances and that you know and are confident about what needs to happen in any given situation.

Sincerely reassuring family members is an important factor in creating a successful relationship. In itself it can also provide really good support to the person. However, if the reassurance is glib or inaccurate, families are likely to feel 'fobbed off' or even excluded and relationships with them may be damaged.

Ways that you can provide reassurance include:

- following the support plan;
- being open and transparent in your communications;
- providing timely and detailed feedback in a way the family would best like to receive it.

4. Rapport

We naturally experience rapport with close friends or those we share an intense interest with. Rapport is a quality of harmony and mutual acceptance that exists between people. Two people in rapport are inclined to give each other the benefit of the doubt and will generally be more patient with each other. When there is rapport it is easier to reach an understanding and to achieve cooperation. It's where communication flows easily.

While rapport is a natural experience it can also be a skill that you can develop and if you do, it will greatly enhance your communication and relationship with a family member. Listening to them and taking a positive interest, and finding areas of common interest, will all help to improve the rapport and therefore the relationship.

With respect, recognition and reassurance you can create an atmosphere where there is a solid platform for rapport to take place.

You can read more about these ideas in *Partnership Working with Family Carers of People with Learning Disabilities and People with Autistic Spectrum Conditions* in this series, by Alison Cowen and Jamie Hanson.

Activity

Go through the 4Rs above: respect, recognition, reassurance and rapport. Write down two examples of how you have worked or could work in this way with the family carers or friends of a person you support. If it is appropriate, talk through your ideas with a family carer or with your manager at your next supervision.

Thinking point

If you work with the advocate of a person you support do you think that the 4Rs apply to that relationship? How would this change the way you worked with an advocate? If you think they don't apply how would you describe good practice in working in partnership with advocates?

Recognising why it is important to work in teams and in partnership with others

The following guidelines will help you see what makes successful partnerships.

Thinking point

Think about two colleagues whom you work with regularly. Why do you think it is important to work in partnership with them? Think of three ways in which you can promote good partnership working.

For support workers, working in partnership with colleagues and other professionals, this means:

- sharing a commitment to providing person centred support for the person;
- being clear about decisions that are made and the reasons for them;

- learning about and respecting other people's roles and responsibilities;

- taking account of opinions and ideas that are different from your own;

- refusing to take part in any situation you recognise as 'unprofessional';

- recognising that you are a member of a team of people with different strengths and talents and being confident in your own worth and ability while not undermining anyone else;

- dealing immediately and directly with any injustice done to you or any colleague or any unprofessional behaviour.

The example below gives an idea of how one support worker, Meena, is promoting partnership working in her day-to-day support of Mita.

Working in partnership

Partnership example	Who is the support worker working in partnership with?	How are they promoting good partnership working?
Mita has recently had a number of chest infections and the doctor has diagnosed asthma. She will need to use an inhaler from now on	Mita and the asthma nurse	Focusing on Mita and her needs, helping her to stay healthy Sharing information in an accessible and culturally sensitive way
The nurse explains to Mita about the inhalers and how to use them. Meena works with Mita and the nurse to explore how best to provide accessible information to Mita and her family so that she can practise at home	Mita and her family and the nurse	Respecting each other's experience and expertise Agreeing a shared plan of action

Partnership working means sharing a commitment to providing person centred support.

Improving partnership working and managing and resolving conflicts

When writing about managing conflict between family carers and support workers, Alison Cowen and Jamie Hanson in their book in this series, *Partnership Working with Family Carers*, identify the following ideas. These can be applied equally to managing conflicts with colleagues and workers from other organisations.

Disagreements and conflicts happen for all sorts of reasons – frequently because people see things very differently depending on their perspective and their role in relation to the person being supported.

In some situations conflict can be constructive – it can help to clarify or resolve important issues or people's roles and it can mean that relatives get involved in significant issues. Conflict can help to release pent-up stress, anxiety or emotion.

On the other hand, conflict can be damaging to relationships and take attention away from important issues. It can damage the morale of both paid staff and family members. Conflict is a major source of stress and illness. Dealing with disagreements and conflict is an important skill in lots of situations.

Activity

Think about a situation you have been involved in or witnessed where there was significant conflict between two people.

- *What was the conflict about?*
- *How were the people communicating?*
- *What emotions did you witness?*
- *How was the conflict ended or resolved?*
- *Who played a major part in resolving the conflict and how did they behave?*
- *What was the relationship between the two people like after the conflict was resolved?*

Important attitudes and skills for resolving conflict include:

- respecting the contribution of others;
- being non judgmental in your approach;
- active listening and communicating openly;
- looking for areas of agreement and seeking a win–win resolution;
- being open and transparent in providing the necessary information for partners;
- being person centred in your approach;
- creativity and flexible thinking.

All of us have to deal with conflict in a whole range of situations and with different people at different times. As a paid worker you need to be aware of your natural style of handling conflict and be aware of other approaches to handling conflict you could use in any situation.

Where you and a family member or colleague disagree it's crucial that you listen to and respect their views even if these are different to your own.

It's crucial that you listen to and respect the views of family members and colleagues.

There are five main styles to handling conflict: competing, accommodating, avoiding, compromising, or joint problem solving. Try to identify which style best represents how you manage conflicts.

1. **Competing** is being assertive and uncooperative. It means an individual pursues their own concerns at the expense of someone else, using whatever power they have to achieve their own ends. Competing might also mean standing up for your rights, defending a position you believe is correct, or just trying to win.

2. **Accommodating** means the person is unassertive and cooperative – virtually giving in. A soothing person tries to preserve the relationship between the parties at all costs, stressing areas of agreement and failing to confront difficult issues.

3. **Avoiding** means the person is unassertive and uncooperative – just not addressing the conflict. Avoiding might be about sidestepping the issue, postponing discussions till a later date or simply withdrawing.

4. **Compromising** comes between assertiveness and cooperativeness. The objective is to find solutions which partially satisfy both parties. It comes between competing and accommodating. It addresses issues more directly than avoiding, but it doesn't explore them in as much depth as in joint

problem solving. Conflict is seen as mutual difference best resolved by cooperation and compromise.

5. **Joint problem solving** is both assertive and cooperative – the opposite of avoiding. It involves working together to identify each other's concerns, learning from each other's insights and finding a solution that meets the concerns of both parties.

Accessing support and advice about partnership working or resolving conflicts

Occasionally partnership working doesn't go as smoothly as we would like. There are misunderstandings or communication breaks down. As a support worker, remember that you don't need to manage any problems you might experience on your own.

Activity

Imagine that you have been supporting Clive for the past six months when he comes to the care farm where you are a support worker. You have developed a good relationship with Bill, his brother, who drops him off on the way to work. One day Bill drops Clive off and is really angry because he didn't know about the trip the following week to the agricultural show, and Clive is upset that he can't go on the trip because of a hospital appointment.

- *What would you do if you were the support worker?*
- *If you are unsure about how to manage the situation who would you ask?*
- *How could you prevent this type of situation happening again?*

If you are unsure about how to manage a conflict in relation to partnership working, or if you need advice about how to progress, then you could ask your line manager or a senior colleague, or you could raise your concerns at a team meeting. Other people may well have experience of managing conflicts that they would be happy to share. Being a reflective worker will help you to learn from your experiences and think about how to approach a similar situation in the future. As in the activity above, in a conflict situation, a support worker needs to respect the contributions of others, listen actively and be person centred in their approach.

Key points from this chapter

- Working in partnership with relatives, friends and advocates of the people you support means respecting their expertise and commitment, recognising their journey, reassuring them about the support you are providing and actively working to build rapport.

- Working in partnership with colleagues means respecting the roles and views of others, communicating clearly and openly, sharing a commitment to supporting the person in a person centred way and constructively challenging poor practice if necessary.

- Reflect on how you generally manage conflict and think about how you can develop your skills in this area.

- If you need support or advice about partnership working or resolving conflicts talk to your line manager or a more experienced colleague.

References and where to go for more information

References

Cowen, A and Hanson, J (2011) *Partnership Working with Family Carers of People with a Learning Disability and People with Autistic Spectrum Conditions.* Kidderminster: BILD

Skills for Care (2010) *Common Core Principles for Working with Family Carers.* Leeds: Skills for Care, downloadable *from* www.skillsforcare.org.uk

Websites

Skills for Care www.skillsforcare.org.uk

Glossary

Advocacy – helping and supporting someone else to speak up for what they want.

Aims – a general statement of what an organisation hopes to achieve.

Code of practice – a UK document for social care workers setting out the standards they should be working to.

Communication – the way that two or more people make contact, build relationships and share messages. These messages can be ideas, thoughts or feelings as well as information and questions. Communication involves both sending and understanding these messages and can be done through many different ways including speech, writing, drawing, pictures, symbols, signs, pointing and body language, for example.

Confidentiality – things that need to be kept private.

Direct payments – a way for people to organise their own social care support by receiving funding direct from their council following an assessment of their needs.

Duty of care – those in a professional or other paid capacity, with responsibility for providing support to others, must take reasonable care to avoid acts or omissions that are likely to cause harm to the person or persons they care for or to other people.

Family carer – a relative of a person with learning disabilities who has an interest in their wellbeing.

General Social Care Council – the organisation that regulates the social care workforce in England and sets the standards of care through the Codes of Practice. In Scotland this is the **Scottish Social Services Council**; in Wales, the **Care Council for Wales/Cyngor Gofal Cymru**; and in Northern Ireland, the **Northern Ireland Social Care Council**.

Informed decision – an informed decision is one where a choice is made by an individual, using relevant information about the advantages and disadvantages of all the possible courses of action.

Induction – a period of learning, shortly after starting a new job or volunteering placement, when workers find out about how to provide good support to people with learning disabilities.

Job description – a document that gives detailed information about your work, what you will be doing, who you are responsible to, etc.

Mental capacity – a person's ability to make their own decisions and to understand the consequences of those decisions.

Neglect – systematically and consistently failing to respond to a person's needs or failing to take actions in their best interests. It can be deliberate, but is not always done on purpose.

Negligence – failure to use reasonable care that would be expected of any other person in a similar situation.

Person centred approach – a way of working every day with people with learning disabilities that puts the person and their dreams at the centre of everything you do.

Personal development plan – a plan completed by a worker with their manager to record their future learning and development needs.

Policy – a statement or plan of action that clearly sets out an organisation's position or approach on a particular issue and tells staff what should be done in the circumstances.

Power – the ability of a person or group of people to exercise authority over another, thereby controlling and influencing others.

Procedure – a set of instructions which sets out in detail how a policy should be implemented and what staff should do in response to a specific situation.

Reflection – careful consideration of ideas and issues.

Rights – a framework of laws that protects people from harm, sets out what people can say and do and guarantees the right to a fair trial and other basic entitlements, such as the right to respect, equality, etc.

Risk – the probability or threat of damage, injury, liability, loss, or other negative occurrence which may be prevented through planned action.

Risk assessment – a careful examination of what could cause harm to people, so that you can weigh up whether you have taken enough precautions or should do more to prevent harm.

Service – the provision of social care support for a person, which could be in their own home, their local community, a residential home or similar place.

Support plan – a detailed plan of a person's support needs that support workers should use to inform their day-to-day support for that individual.

Index

Added to a page number 'g' denotes glossary.